I0002338

IPHONE 12 BEGINNER GUIDE

10 NEW TRICKS TO HAVE A FUN USER EXPERIENCE

By **JOHN CONTON**

Copyright ©2020

All rights reserved
This book is for public consumption, any
reseduction of any parts of this book must be
done with written permission from the
publisher.

ACKNOWLEDGEMENT

I wish to acknowledge the makers and owners of the device that will be discussed in this book

DEDICATION

To my dearest tech geeks all over the world.

INTRODUCTION

Hello to you my name is John, and i know you just got your brand-new iphone 12. You probably went through the initial setup process but now you're wondering how you can get the most out of your brand new iPad pro. Do not worry, this book was put together all for you, so you can make out the most out of your device.

There are several tweaks and things you must have to do on your device to have that awesome user experience and I will reveal them all here, so lets dig in.

TABLE OF CONTENTS

ABOUT THE iphone 12

First of all, some basic information about the iphone 12 we are learning about. There are several awesome additions to this latest edition of iphone from the previous edition, and one of the most senounced feature in the iphone 12 is the addition of the usingle lens camera.

Other new features includes:

1. Upgraded microphone.

2. Quality 6 gigs of ram across the board.

3. Wi-Fi 6.

4. 64-512 GB of storage.

5. The new Lidar scanner

6. A14 Bionic processesor chip, which is the fastest chip in a smartphone and a 120 Hz refresh rate.

Furthermore, the screen of the device is protected by Scratch-resistant glass and oleophobic coating.

The front camera has a 12 MP (wide). The phone's sensors include Siri natural language commands, Face ID, gyro, proximity, compass, barometer and dictation. accelerometer,

PERSONAL REVIEW OF THE IPHONE 12 2020

So let me give me my honest review about the iphone 12. Note that this is **MY** opinion.

So starting with the single lens camera, to be honest it doesn't matter to me at all as I take my photos with my iphone which already has an ultra wide lens. But if you don't have the newer models of iphone with this feature, then this a very nice buy for you.

About the microphone quality, this is actually something that could be useful for anyone doing online zoom meetings or for those who want to record podcasts.

For the RAM, I'm glad that Apple decided to give the 2020 iphone 12 a 6 gigabytes of RAM, since a major focus of the iphone is now multitasking. So this is one of the biggest advantages compared to the previous iphones in the lineup, this will definitely help for seductivity work like photo and video editing as well. This makes the functionality of the device quite fast. This will make the device download apps and install games quickly, it will make multitasking easy, and it wont buffer during or video calls of while playing games. And of course, a more efficient prosecessor is good for batteries.

The WiFi 6 is a nice little addition, but it's important to note that it really only makes a difference if your house is set up with the Wi-Fi 6 internet router. So if you don't plan on getting one of these routers any time soon, then it really shouldn't matter to you.

About the increased storage, upto 512 gigs of storage is probably the biggest deal that you'll notice about the 2020 iphone 12, I think 512 gigs of storage is going to help a lot of people for storing files, apps, photos and game

Talking about new Lidar scanner. This is remote sensing technology that's typically used in aircraft, mapping vehicles, and self-driving cars. This is a very interesting addition because it greatly imseves the accuracy of an object and depth tracking

12

which is used for augmented reality apps. However there just aren't very many compelling air apps out right now so chances are you won't have much use for it for a while but I think Apple is actually looking towards the future by adding lidar.

SIGN IN YOUR APPLE ID

First of all before we start, the most basic thing that you will have to do is to log in or sign in to your iphone with your Apple account details. Without that, you won't be able to easily share data between your iphone and your other Apple devices, and other features like Sidecar mode won't work either.

Guidelines For Sign In

1. Tap and go to your Settings.

2. Tap Sign in to your iphone.

3. Enter your Apple ID email address. If you don't have don't have one? The next steps are the guidelines to do so

- Click on "Don't have an Apple ID or forgot it"

- Click on Create Apple ID.

- Click. Enter your first and last name and birthdate in the spaces shown .

- Click Next.

- In the 'Email Address' screen, click on "Don't have an email address?" button

- Click Get an iCloud Email Address.

- From the 'Email Address' screen enter your email then click Next. This email address will become your Apple ID.

- Click on Create Email Address to confirm.

- Enter your preferred password into the required fields.

- The Password must be at least 8 characters, including a number and an uppercase and lowercase letter

- Click and 'Phone Number' screen, tap Continue.

- You will have to review the Terms and Conditions.

- Click on agree to confirm.

- You will be sent an email with verification steps in the email address you entered.

- After that, you can then sign

4. Enter your password and click Next.

 You're signed into your iphone!

Apple might ask you to upgrade your account security. I would recommend this because 2-factor authentication is a good security assurance anytime.

GETTING FAMILIAR WITH THE GESTURE CONTROL

What is Gesture Control?

The gesture control feature is a nice feature that allows the user to control the iphone and its apps using a few simple finger gestures to perform tasks such as

- Tap
- Swipe
- Scroll
- Touch and Hold
- Zoom

How the Fingers work with Gesture Control

1. You can tap one finger lightly on the screen to wake the device or open an app.

2. You can quickly swipe one finger or two over the screen of your device to move over to the next page or move left or right.

3. You can move one finger up and down the screen of your device to scroll up and down. This is called scrolling.

4. You can use a finger to touch and hold items in an app or in Control Center to check out contents before opening, sort of a preview and perform some quick actions. Also, if you are on the Home screen, you can touch and hold an app icon briefly to open a preview menu screen.

5. You can you the gesture control to zoom in and out

Once you unbox your iphone , the first thing you to should do is get familiar with the **gesture control**. This feature is available in older iphones, but incase this is the very first iphone you are using without a home button then you are going to have to learn how to navigate throughout the Apple operating system (iOS) without having that home button.

Its good to note that the gestures are going to be very similar to how they are on the iphone 10, 10s, X, Xmax, 11 and 11se. So basically, if you swipe down from the top right, you always see that you have the control center right there, if you swipe down from the top middle or the top left or anywhere besides the top right, it will be your Notification Center and you can also see the time and everything right there.

If you swipe up from the bottom and hold that's how you can get into the multitasking mode. You can also see where all your windows are open and you can go ahead and scroll in to see all of your open applications. You can also do that by using four fingers - kind of pinching in – to do so.

For the multitasking, if you go into an application like Facebook, and you wanted to have another application side by side and do multitasking, all you have to do is to swipe up from the bottom to bring up the dock and then you can use both applications at the same time side by side. For you to get home, just swipe up from the bottom - you can also use the four fingers as well- to get home.

Lastly about the gesture feature, the last gesture I want to teach you is how to get in and out of applications quickly. How to do this is by swiping on the bottom bar so you can get in and out of applications very quickly. By swiping on the home bar down at the bottom of your iphone is the quickest way to do weave in and out of applications seamlessly. This is sebably the most used gesture besides just going home on my iphone 11 Se, so this is definitely a function that you're going to want to get familiar with and use it a lot because it makes everything very quick, it makes you be able to basically fly through iOS you can get in and out of applications just very quickly.

I hope I made this clear enough and you understood it.

ALTERNATIVE APPEARANCE

Alternative Appearance allows you as a user to set up another Face ID of yourself Incase you may be confined to look a certain way at some point of your every day, or if there is anybody else you might want to authorize to gain access to your iphone 12.

So if you want multiple people to have access to your device, or if you just look completely different if you wear something on your face or on your head, you could set up an alternate appearance right there. You also have the options to use face ID for iphone unlock for the app store, for Apple pay and also password autofill. I would highly suggest having all of these enabled.

For you to use this option, you will have to setup the Require Attention feature. As you scroll down, you can see "the require attention from face ID" button, there you have the attention aware features there as well. You can also see the options as you scroll down, those options will give you access to certain things when the device is locked, so you can go and configure the options to your preference.

Having face ID on your iphone is just awesome, and the reasons for this have been stated earlier   but the   password autofill feature is sebably my favorite feature to use face ID. I know you can use touch ID to carry out your activities but it just seems to be a lot quicker with face ID and password autofill. The feature allows you to use your face ID to log in sites and app by autofilling the the password that you inputted. For instance if you go into the Safari app, then onto a login page, you can see the passwords button, if you do have a password, all you have to do is simply tap on that it will scan your face ID and then it will log you in . Password autofill is definitely one of my favorite features with any kind of face ID enabled device including this brand new iphone 12 so definitely make sure you have that set up in the face ID and passcode settings .

The guidelines are:

1. Click Settings

2. Scroll   down and tap Passwords & Accounts.

3. Tap AutoFill Passwords

4. Toggle next to AutoFill Passwords.

5. You'll also want to turn your iCloud Keychai on if you haven't do so.

DISPLAY SETTINGS

To configure your display

1. Click Settings

2. Click Display and Brightness Panel

Enable or Disable True Tone

From this button you can go ahead and enable or disable true tone. I actually prefer to have true tone you can try it with and without.

For the Lock Settings

You can definitely change out of lock from two minutes to either like 10 to 15 minutes, or even to "never" if you forget to lock your device. Definitely set this to never just because you don't want to be like reading a long article of like 5 paragraphs inside of Safari and be stuck and then your device just locks, it's really annoying so I would definitely rather have you leave it at 10 to 15 minutes or Never.

Display Zoom Settings

1. Click on the Display Settings

2. Click on the Display Zoom Settings . You now can see you the display zoom settings.

Display zoom is usually good for people bad eyesight or for senior citizens. So if you want your screen to be zoomed in more than the standard or if you have bad eyes, then you have to definitely check this out.

Auto Brightness

1. Click on the Display Settings

2. Click on General accessibility

3. Display accommodation. In this settings, you can see auto-brightness. You can turn it off or you could turn it that on or off. I prefer to have mine disabled

Frame rate

You also have limit framerate settings in the scroll down. If you want to adjust the framerate or if you want to kind of clock it out or max it out, maybe like say at 60 frames per second, you can enable it using the frame rate setting right there. This feature ensures that your iphone will never have a frame rate of anything over 60.

APPLE PENCIL

The new Apple pencil feature was first launched in the 2018 iphone 12, so if you have used the 2018 iphone this might not be too hard for you to get around. But if this your first time of using a device that has this apple pencil feature, then you should connect it and get familiar with how works.

The first biggest change is that it actually attaches to the top or the side depending on which orientation you're in the screen of the iphone. You can wirelessly charge it. Once you take it off, you can use it just normally. One thing to note is that you cannot actually go home or use any of the gestures or with the pencil. I should say so it's a little bit annoying that you can't you know go home or hold down the control center and things like that with the Apple pencil. But you do have to use your finger sometimes because it's a pencil, you know it's not really a stylus but if we go into an application like notes, and if you double tap there are gestures so you can erase so if I double tap again it will

27

take you back to pencil and you can draw with it.

For settings of Apple pencil, you can see it in the settings button. You can switch between current tool and eraser. You can have it where it switches between the current tool and last tool used, or you can also change the settings so it shows the color palette.

You can turn the DoubleTap feature off which I'd highly not recommend so I like to keep mine at the default which is the current tool and eraser. But if you will use this in other applications, which I'm sure later on there are going to be more applications that implement compatibility with the DoubleTap feature on the new Apple penci, then I'd recommend trying it out and learning it. Anyways, if you' would be only using this for drawing and just handwriting, I would definitely suggest you use tool and eraser tool.

APPS INSTALLATION

There are different type of apps you might need for the efficient functioning of your device. In this age and time, social media apps might top the table of those apps you might want to install from the Apple store.

Social media applications are very vital to modern and today's way of communication with our friends and family, so it's recommended you install social media apps on your device. Depending on your preferred services or the websites or apps you have been using in your previous devices you would have to download these social media apps from the Apple store. Apps like Facebook App, Twitter App, YouTube App, Instagram App, Snapchat App etc. So head over to the Apple Store and start installing these applications on your device.

There are a lot of awesome games you can install too and applications that are just for the iphone, so you should definitely go into the App Store and explore around some of the iphone applications. Once you've installed those applications, go back to your home screen and start organizing them on your home screen.

One application that i would recommend you install is a calculator since there is no calculator built in to the iphone for some reason which we don't know for now. You should definitely install a calculator application.

ORGANIZING YOUR APPS ON YOUR HOME SCREEN

You will have to organize your apps manually one by one to get them to fit to your preferred location you want them to be. It's recommended to pin the apps you would be using more often where they would be very easily accessible to tap on.

So how to do this:

Tap and hold the app you want to move. Then move the app by moving it around on the home screen and then place it where you want it to be. You can also move it down to the dock. A dock allows you to fit a lot of applications down inside of it. If you want to move multiple apps at a time, just go and tap on that while it's in wiggle mode you can see you can move multiple applications at once. This is a nice feature anyways, so just move them around like that, if you can create a folder where you can just put them on top of each other.

You should organize your dock as this is where most of your important applications are going to be. So you have to put all of your most important applications down there. On the right of the dock is going to be your most userd or your recently used applications, you can actually disable this feature if you want to but actually I'd recommend you leave it that way because it does give you access to recently used applications that you may not have in the dock and they may not be as easy to access so.

Like I mentioned earlier, you could just pull an application down from the home screen into the dock and you can move them out the same way as well. However i recommend you should definitely change it from the default look, you can definitely customize it to whatever applications you use the most because once again this is what you're going to be able to get into when you're inside of other applications. If you pull up the dock like that you can get to all these applications without going back to the home screen and by the way if you wanted to disable those recently used applications if it go into settings multitasking in dock you can see down here show suggested in recent apps you could turn that off if you do not want that you also have these other settings you can take a look at as well.

BATTERY AND SCREEN TIME CHART

One important knowledge you have to know about your iphone is getting familiar with the battery and the screen time charts inside of settings. How to do this:

1. Go into settings

2. Go to battery.

Here, this is going to show you a great breakdown of the way your battery life is actually being used. So it's going to show you which applications are using up the most of your battery life. You can get very specific with this by clicking on the bar chart at certain hours and it will show you from 12:00 to 1:00 p.m. You can click on the top chart as well if you want to and it breaks it down by the hour and then of course you can get an average over the last 10 days which is really useful .

Basically, if you click on the show settings, you can see it shows what your most used applications are today and over the last 7 days. It can also show how long you've been using those applications.

DOWNTIME

Downtime is a feature which allows you schedule time away from your screen. You can also set limits for applications incase you have your kids getting on your iphone or if you actually bought the device for them.

You definitely want to check out app limits and applications that are allowed as well you can also check out the privacy restriction so you can block certain websites and certain applications and then of course you can use a passcode to get into the actual screen time settings. What you definitely want to do if you have kids who are maybe a little bit older and smart enough to figure out how to disable some of these features in here. So definitely play around with it, there's a lot to see and a lot to do inside of screen time.

ENHANCING BATTERY LIFE

You may want to tweak around your iphone to minimize the wastage of battery life. There are features you might not totally need for the functionality of your device, so you might want to disable or turn off those features. So these tweaks include:

1. Disabling email fetch and email push.

    a) Go to settings

    b) Go to mail, you want to find your account

    c) Then disable fetch and push.

Make sure that you get your mail manually every time you go into the application, that's the only time it's going to refresh. Others include

    1. You can also disable significant locations and you will need to put in your face ID.

2. You can disable routing in traffic, personally for me because i'm never going to use this for know GPS or anything like that.

3. You can also disable the popular near me feature.

4. You can also disable iphone analytics.

5. You would want to make sure that things like the weather application are also disabled if you really don't have need for that.

FIND IPHONE

You can also put on the Find My iphone, just in case you do get your iphone stolen or it gets lost. With that you will be able to track down your device.

CONTROL CENTER CONFIGURATION

One important thing you should do is to configure your control center and also your widgets.

So starting with the control center, you can get there from swiping down on the top right of the screen. You can see that are all these different toggles right here and you can also add a 3d touch. On these to get more options, you get 3d touch on the platter right on the top of the screen.

Guidelines

1. Go into the settings.

2. Scroll down to settings for control center.

3. Click on customize controls. This is where you can add in other toggles.

4. If you want to add something you have to just click on the plus icon right there and it will show up right away so you can see we have that added in right there. If you

wanted to move it around you can do and you can see it will change in real time, which is pretty cool feature. And then of course if you wanted to delete it you can click on the red button and it will delete it.

5. For Widgets Settings, go to your home screen and swipe over so you can see the widget section. From there, you can see the edit button right and that is where you can add and remove certain widgets, you can also move them around by clicking and dragging over to move the position of the actual widget and you have all the other widgets down here that you can add them.

You can also get more widgets for the applications you install, so if you install an application that supports widgets, you can configure these to your liking.

USING SHORTCUTS

Go to the Apple Store and download series shortcuts from the App Store.

So go to the App Store and just search for shortcuts, you will see series shortcuts in there, definitely go ahead and download it. This is one of my favorite features by far if not my favorite feature overall in iOS 13, so of course you're a big fan of multitasking and just automating and getting things done quickly, then this is very good for you.

UPGRADING YOUR iCLOUD STORAGE

One thing you should do is to consider upgrading your iCloud storage plan to make room for other things on your iphone.

The iphone 12 has upto 256 GB memory ROM, depending on the version you buy, which is quite large but if you are somebody that has loads of files on iCloud like me, all my storage is basically offloaded onto iCloud; google drives, photos and things like that. Then you might want to get more storage space for your files on your iphone.

How to do this:

a. Click on iCloud

b. Click on iCloud settings.

c. Click on manage storage.

You can see the various storage plans.

✓ 5 GB for $0

- ✓ 50 GB for $0.99

- ✓ 200 GB for $2.99

- ✓ 2 TB for $9.99

I would go ahead and consider upgrading your iCloud storage plan just so you can make room for things like movies. And you know if you want have music on your device, I would recommend actually not downloading music onto your device but paying for streaming services like Spotify or Apple music, that way you don't take up a ton of storage on your device. You don't really need to download movies either because you do have the offline feature inside of Netflix but you might be downloading movies to watch while you are traveling and things like that so need all these storage.

USING USB TYPE C TO CHARGE YOUR IPHONE FROM YOUR IPHONE

It's good to know that USBC to lightning cable to be able to charge your iphone from your iphone 12. So as you know that the iphone 12 now uses USB C to charge and that means that you could actually plug in a USB C charger to lightning charger and charge your iphone or any iphone with the Lightning port from the USBC connector of the iphone.

Note that I have not personally tried this so I don't know how much drains the battery of the iphone itself. I will have to test that in the future but this could be a great way to charge your iphone if there's no an outlet nearby or anything like that or if you don't have a portable charger, this is a great way to be able to do.

THE END

www.ingramcontent.com/pod-product-compliance
Lightning Source LLC
LaVergne TN
LVHW010041070326
832903LV00071B/4682